3.95

12/05

ITALY

LETTERS FROM AROUND THE WORLD

Fiona Tankard

Photographs by Sue Cunningham

CHERRYTREE BOOKS

LETTERS FROM AROUND THE WORLD

Distributed in the United States by
Cherrytree Books
1980 Lookout Drive
North Mankato, MN 56001

U.S. publication copyright © Cherrytree Books 2005

Library of Congress Cataloging-in-Publication Data
Tankard, Fiona.
  Italy / by Fiona Tankard.
    p.cm. – (Letters from around the world)
  First published: London : Evans Brothers, 2002.
  Includes bibliographical references and index.
  ISBN 1-84234-247-9 (alk. paper)
   1. Italy--Juvenile literature. 2. Italy--Social life and
  customs--Juvenile literature. 3.
  Children--Italy--Social life and customs--Juvenile
  literature. 4.
  Children--Italy--Correspondence--Juvenile literature.
  I. Title. II. Series.

DG451.T26 2004
945--dc22

                       2004041449

First published in 2002 by
Evans Brothers Ltd
2A Portman Mansions
Chiltern Street
London W1U 6NR
United Kingdom
Copyright © Evans Brothers 2002

Conceived and produced by

Nutshell
MEDIA

www.nutshellmedialtd.co.uk

Editor: Katie Orchard
Design: Mayer Media Ltd
Cartography: Encompass Graphics Ltd
Artwork: Mayer Media Ltd
Consultants: Jeff Stanfield and Anne Spiring
All photographs were taken by Sue Cunningham.

Printed in China

Acknowledgments
The author would like to thank the following for their help: the Cesaroni family; the principal, staff, and students of the Elementary School, Vaiano.

Cover: Matteo and his soccer friends.
Title page: Matteo with his friends Marco, Lorenzo, and Lucrezia.
This page: The *scuolabus* on its way to school.
Contents page: Matteo's grandpa at work on his tractor.
Glossary page: Matteo's class and teacher.
Further information page: Matteo lights the bread oven.
Index: Matteo goes for a bike ride.

Contents

My Country

Monday, January 7

Via Trasimeno 14
Poggi
06062 Castiglione del Lago
Italy

Dear Joe,

Ciao! (pronounced "chow." This means "hi" or "bye" in Italian.)

I'm Matteo Cesaroni and I'm eight years old. I live in Poggi (pronounced "podgy"), a small village in Umbria, in central Italy. I have two sisters, Vanessa, who is 10, and Chiara, who is five.

Being pen pals will be great fun. Hurry up and write back soon!

From

Matteo

This is what I look like. Grandma, Dad, Vanessa, Mom, Chiara, and Grandpa are all on the balcony.

Italy lies in southern Europe, between the Mediterranean and Adriatic Seas.

Italy's place in the world.

Some people say that Italy looks like a boot kicking a ball. The country is divided into many regions. Umbria is one of them.

Umbria is a quiet and beautiful region. One of its most famous towns is Assisi, where St. Francis lived. Umbria is very popular with tourists.

Like much of Italy, there are many villages in Umbria. Many young people are now choosing to move to cities to find work.

Behind Matteo's house there are fields, olive trees, and rows of vines.

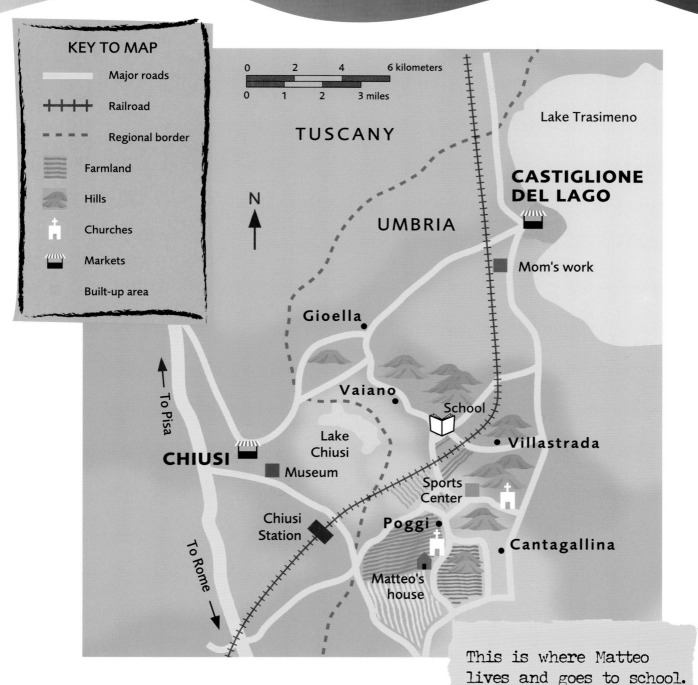

KEY TO MAP

▬▬▬▬	Major roads
┼┼┼┼	Railroad
‑ ‑ ‑ ‑	Regional border
〰〰	Farmland
🌄	Hills
✝	Churches
🏪	Markets
▪	Built-up area

TUSCANY

Lake Trasimeno

CASTIGLIONE DEL LAGO

Mom's work

UMBRIA

Gioella

N

To Pisa

Vaiano

School

Lake Chiusi

CHIUSI

Museum

Villastrada

Sports Center

Poggi

Chiusi Station

To Rome

Matteo's house

Cantagallina

This is where Matteo lives and goes to school.

Poggi means "hills" in Italian and the village has lots of hills surrounding it.
The nearest big town is Chiusi, which is 4 miles (7 km) away. Castiglione del Lago is another large town. It is 9 miles (15 km) away. Matteo's family goes to the market there on Wednesdays.

Landscape and Weather

Umbria is a mountainous region. Its landscape is a patchwork of vineyards, olive groves, woods, and fields. It also has the largest lake in central Italy, called Lake Trasimeno.

Grandpa plows a field to make it ready for planting winter wheat.

The climate in northern Italy is cooler and wetter than in the south. Central Italy is hot in summer. In the winter it can be quite cold. Sometimes the mountains become covered in snow and people go there to ski.

Vanessa with olives grown on the farm. They are pressed to make olive oil.

Umbria's Climate

January

Temperature
41 °F
(5 °C)

Rainfall
3 in (76 mm)

July

Temperature
77 °F
(25 °C)

Rainfall
1–2 in
(43 mm)

At Home

Matteo's family lives in an old farmhouse. His grandparents live there, too. The original building is nearly 200 years old. As the Cesaroni family has grown, new rooms have been added to the building.

Long ago, cows used to live downstairs. The heat from their bodies kept the people upstairs warm.

This is the farmhouse. Matteo lives downstairs.

Now the house has been turned into two apartments. Matteo's grandparents live in the one upstairs and Matteo's family lives on the ground floor.

Grandpa and Matteo plant some garlic. Grandma uses garlic to flavor their food.

Matteo's family has three cats and three dogs. This is Chiara with her kitten, Stella.

Matteo adds wood to the bread oven.

Each apartment in the farmhouse has a kitchen, bathroom, living room, and three bedrooms. There is also a pantry, or *cantina*, to store the food that the family grows.

Not all homes in the area are like Matteo's. There are also modern houses and small apartment buildings.

Grandma in the *cantina* with her special tomato sauce.

Monday, April 15

Via Trasimeno 14
Poggi
06062 Castiglione del Lago
Italy

Dear Joe,

It was great to get your letter last week. Did I tell you we've got a bread oven outside our house? My job is to gather bits of wood for it from around the farm. We use it for barbecues, or to cook Grandma's delicious pizzas.

Yesterday after lunch, Vanessa, Chiara, and I played with our karaoke machine. It was great fun. I've got a good voice—well, I think so anyway!

Ciao,

Matteo

I love our karaoke machine, even though Vanessa says I sound like one of our cats!

Food and Mealtimes

On school days Matteo wakes up at 6:30 A.M. For breakfast he has hot milk with a little coffee in it and a *brioche*, a sweet cake. During the morning he usually has a snack of fruit or sometimes *bruschetta*, toasted bread with olive oil and garlic.

Grandma picks vegetables from the garden.

Matteo buys fresh bread from Domenico, the bread man.

Vegetables for sale in the weekly market at Castiglione del Lago.

Matteo buys bread from the bread van, which comes to the house every day. Most of the family's vegetables are grown at home. The rest are bought from the local market.

Lunch is the main meal. It starts with pasta, maybe spaghetti or tagliatelle (flat spaghetti) with sauce. Next Matteo eats roast meat and vegetables. Afterward he has fresh fruit from the orchard.

In the autumn, chestnuts are a special treat. Uncle Fabio is heating some for Chiara.

Sometimes Matteo's family has pizza for dinner.

Friday, June 7

Via Trasimeno 14
Poggi
06062 Castiglione del Lago
Italy

Ciao Joe!

My grandma makes the best tagliatelle! Here's her recipe:

You will need: 3 cups plain flour, 1 quart of water,
3 large eggs, pinch of salt

1. Add the eggs and salt to the flour and mix with a fork.
2. Now mix everything together with your hands until it becomes a dough.
3. Knead the dough until it is smooth and stretchy. Leave it for 15 minutes to "rest."
4. Roll the dough out on a floured board until it is $1/16$ inch thick and cut it into $1/4$-inch-wide strips.
5. Cook the tagliatelle in 1 quart of boiling salted water for about 3—5 minutes.

It's delicious with hot tomato sauce! Try it and let me know if you like it.

From

Matteo

Grandma and I making tagliatelle.

School Day

Matteo goes to the primary school in Vaiano, a village 2 miles (3 km) away. Most pupils travel to school by car or on the *scuolabus* (school bus). At about 7:15 A.M. Matteo catches the *scuolabus* outside his house.

Matteo's *scuolabus* picks up children from all the villages on the way to Vaiano.

This is Matteo's class during an English lesson.

School starts at 8 A.M. with assembly and finishes at 12:30 P.M. Twice a week, school finishes at 4:30 P.M. Matteo has lessons in math, history, science, geography, religious studies, Italian, and English.

Matteo's teacher, Paolo, helps him to use the computer.

Matteo has lunch in the cafeteria.

In Italy, children start school at the age of six. Matteo will stay at primary school until he is 11 years old. Then he will go to middle school. He will go to high school when he is 14.

After school, Matteo and some of his friends play soccer.

Wednesday, September 18

Via Trasimeno 14
Poggi
06062 Castiglione del Lago
Italy

Hi Joe,

I'm glad you liked the tagliatelle! At school today we played a game called "Odds and Evens." You should try it. Here's how to play:

1. Each player guesses "odd" or "even."
2. Players shake their fists in time to this song:

   > Let's throw them down
   > At eleven o'clock –
   > One, two, three...

3. On "three" everyone holds out between zero and 10 fingers. Add them up. The winner is the one who guessed "odd" or "even" correctly.

What do you do during recess? Write back and tell me.

Ciao,

Matteo

Here are my friends Francesco, Antonio, and Tomaso playing "Odds and Evens."

Off to Work

Matteo's dad works for a building company. He delivers building materials all over the area in his truck. Sometimes he has to drive very long distances.

Matteo's dad with his truck.

Matteo's mom serves a customer at the supermarket checkout.

Matteo's mom works as a cashier at a supermarket in Castiglione del Lago. She is also in charge of ordering the food that the store sells.

In Umbria, many people are farmers. The area is also very popular with vacationers, so some people work in hotels and campgrounds.

A hotel receptionist welcomes a tourist to the area.

Free Time

There is always plenty to do on the farm. Matteo's dad spends much of his free time driving the tractor or repairing farm machinery.

Matteo helps his dad fix the tractor.

Matteo's favorite ride at the fair is the bumper cars.

When the farm work is done, Matteo's dad and Uncle Fabio sometimes go fishing on the lake. Matteo's mom likes to go to dancing classes with her friends.

The big, all-year fair at Perugia is Matteo's favorite place to go on weekends. He also enjoys riding his bike with friends.

The country roads around Poggi are fun and safe places for bike riding.

Religion

Matteo's house has a small statue of the Madonna beside the window.

Most Italians are Roman Catholics, but Italy has several other religions, too.

Matteo's family is Roman Catholic. When Matteo is 10 years old, he will take lessons to prepare him for his First Communion.

Matteo's family visits the little church in Poggi.

Sunday, November 3

Via Trasimeno 14
Poggi
06062 Castiglione del Lago
Italy

Dear Joe,

Yesterday it was the Day of the Dead. We took chrysanthemums to my great-grandma's grave in the cemetery at Villastrada. It's traditional here to visit our relatives' graves on this day or on November 1, All Saints' Day.

Italy has lots of festivals. My favorite is Ferragosto, on August 15, when everyone has a day off and all the stores are closed. What's your favorite festival?

Ciao,

Matteo

Mom always puts flowers in the special flower holder for my great-grandma.

Fact File

Capital City: Rome is a very old city. There are many ancient buildings, including the Colosseum, where gladiators used to fight.

There is also a small independent state inside Rome, called Vatican City. This is where the Pope lives.

Other Major Cities:
Florence, Venice, and Pisa (home of the Leaning Tower of Pisa).

Neighboring Countries:
France, Switzerland, Austria, and Slovenia.

Size: 115,811 square miles (301,278 km²).

Population: 57,784,000.

Currency:
The euro (€). This replaced the Italian lire in January 2002. There are 100 cents in a euro. It is now the currency used by 12 of the 15 members of the European Union.

It costs 41 cents (0.41 euros) to send a letter within Europe.

Flag: The Italian flag is based on the French flag, which has a blue stripe instead of a green one. This design was brought to Italy by Napoleon in 1797.

Languages: Italian is the official language. Some people also speak French, German, and Slovene on the borders.

Main Industries: Tourism, machinery, iron and steel, chemicals, cars, clothes, footwear, ceramics.

Longest River: The River Po, 404 miles (652 km). It is in the north.

Highest Mountain: Monte Bianco (Mont Blanc), 15,767 feet (4,807 m). This is in the Alps in northern Italy.

Famous Italians:
Leonardo da Vinci painted the world's most famous painting, the *Mona Lisa*. He was born in Italy in 1452. He was an engineer, sculptor, painter, and architect. Other famous Italians include Galileo Galilei, born in 1564, who among other things invented a type of telescope, and Guglielmo Marconi, born in 1874, who invented the radio.

Famous Foods: Italy is most famous for foods such as ice cream, pizza, and pasta. There are more than 300 kinds of pasta in Italy!

Main Religions: Roman Catholicism is the main religion, but there is also Protestantism and Judaism. Catholic Italians celebrate Christmas and Easter. They have several other public holidays, including Epiphany on January 6. This is also the day when Italian children expect a visit from the Epiphany witch, who brings presents if they have been good and leaves coal if they have been bad!

Glossary

All Saints' Day A Christian festival on November 1 to honor all the saints in the Christian Church.

brioche (pronounced "bree-osh") A small, rounded sweet roll.

bruschetta (pronounced "broo-sket-ta") Toasted bread with olive oil and garlic.

cantina A room where dried, canned, or bottled food is stored.

ciao (pronounced "chow") This can mean "hello" or "bye."

Colosseum A big, circular building in Rome with seats around an arena, built between A.D. 75 and A.D. 80.

Day of the Dead A special prayer day on November 2 when people pray for the dead.

Epiphany This is the celebration of the coming of the three wise men after Jesus was born. It is always on January 6.

European Union A group of 15 countries in Europe that work and trade together.

First Communion The time when a young person can take a full part in the Catholic mass. He or she can then receive the holy bread and wine.

gladiators Men who were trained to fight in arenas to entertain people in ancient Roman times. They fought either each other or wild animals.

karaoke machine A machine that plays the tunes of popular songs, while you sing the words.

Madonna Another name for the Virgin Mary.

Pope The head of the Roman Catholic Church.

tagliatelle (pronounced "tal-ya-tel-leh") Tagliatelle is pasta shaped in long, thin strips.

Further Information

Information books:

Pirotta, Saviour. *A Flavour of Italy*. Hodder & Stoughton Children's Division, 2002.

Harvey, Miles. *Games People Play: Italy*. Children's Press, 1996.

Martin, Fred. *Next Stop: Italy*. Heinemann Library, 1998.

Pluckrose, Henry. *Picture a Country: Italy*. Franklin Watts, 1998.

Kelley, Gary. *T is for Toscana*. Creative Editions, 2003.

Fiction:

MacDonell, Annie (ed). *Biancabella and Other Italian Fairy Tales*. Dover Publications, 2001.

Arnold McCully, Emily. *The Orphan Singer*. Arthur A. Levine Books, 2001.

Middleton, Haydn. *We're on our way to Italy*. Scholastic, 2000.

De Paola, Tomie. *The Legend of Old Befana*. Voyager, 1989.

Web sites:

CIA World Factbook
www.cia.gov/cia/publications /factbook/
Basic facts and figures about Italy and other countries.

In Italy Online
www.initaly.com/
General travel information about Italy.

Giardino Italiano
http://www.giardino.it/junior/
Web site made by children for children around the world, with links to Italian pen pals.

Index